*T*he

of the

*O*nly *G*od

The Colourpoint Logo

The Colourpoint is one of the most beautiful of all the long-haired cat breeds. Persian in temperament and shape, it has the coloured points of the Siamese on the face, ears, paws and tail. The Colourpoint logo depicts a real blue-cream point kitten, Lady Jane Grey, and was drawn by Rhoda McClure, a fifth form art student at Omagh Academy, Co. Tyrone.

The *H*arper

of the

Only God

A selection of poetry by

Alice Milligan

Edited by
Sheila Turner
Johnston

COLOURPOINT PRESS

COLOURPOINT PRESS
Omagh Business Complex
Gortrush
Omagh
Co Tyrone
BT78 5LS

Poems © Milligan estate

This edition © Colourpoint Press
1993

ISBN   1 898392 05 6

Cover design by Typeform Repro, Dublin
Layout and design by Sheila Johnston
Typeset by Colourpoint Press
Film output by Typeform Repro, Dublin
Printed by ColourBooks, Dublin

This book has received support from the Cultural Traditions
Programme of the Community Relations Council, which aims to
encourage acceptance and understanding of cultural diversity.

Illustrations:
Cover   - *The Death of Cuchulain* by Oliver Sheppard.
                             Photograph courtesy of An Post.
Alice as a young girl - Courtesy of Methodist College, Belfast.
Alice in old age   - Courtesy of Milligan estate

Colourpoint Press gratefully acknowledges assistance from the Irish
and Local Studies Library of the Western Education and Library
Board in the preparation of this book.

CONTENTS

Alice Milligan's school photograph,
taken at Methodist College, Belfast

Alice Milligan, aged about
seventy-six.

INTRODUCTION

This little volume is long overdue if only as an inadequate token gesture to an influential figure in a critical period of Ireland's past. None of Alice Milligan's poetry has been published in book form since 1954.

Born in 1866 she lived for nearly eighty-seven years, long enough to have seen plenty of both glory and tragedy, personally and on a national level; long enough also to be described by Thomas McDonagh in 1908 as Ireland's greatest living Irish poet.

Although she wrote prose and drama as well as verse, it was as a poet that she described herself. On a wartime travel permit she cites her occupation as "writer (verse)".

Her poems reflect a life which was broad in personal experience and narrow in political aspiration. As a Northern Protestant advocate of the Home Rule cause 100 years ago she has risked being stereotyped as a political writer.

This is a shame.

Undeniably she was a vehement propagandist, but it is my deliberate intention to show the breadth of her talent as a writer of humour and sensitivity, one who valued friendship and love as much as patriotism.

The poems in this book make no pretence to be anything other than a representative miscellany. They are very much my personal choice and include many verses that are not in the 1954 "Poems" (published by Gill and Son).

The selection is quite deliberately mixed. Like a pack of cards thrown in the air, they are printed as they fell (with the sole exception of the six poems in memory of Marjorie Arthur). For this is a book for dipping into, for sampling Alice Milligan's legacy in all its variety.

I would ask the reader to remember only one thing. Alice's style and language are that of the late 19th century and early 20th century. So are her politics. If you superimpose upon her any prejudgements formed by events in late 20th century Ireland you do her a great disservice. She is not here now to give her opinions, so let us leave her in her own day or leave her alone.

Sheila Johnston
Omagh
8th October 1993

PUBLISHER'S NOTE

For those who would like to read further about Alice's long and remarkable life, **Colourpoint Press** intends to publish her biography in Spring 1994.

THE HARPER OF THE ONLY GOD

AT the hour of midnight, a time of full moon,
Cuchulain lay, but slept not, on a couch of the dun;
Winds were not breathing, waters were still;
There came a sound of harping across the hill.

The first notes of that harping, they were soft and low
As the voice of his dear love of long ago;
The next notes rang clearly as a triumph call
On a red field of conflict when champions fall.

At the first notes of the music his eyes grew dim;
At the next, the rage of battle arose in him;
He leaps to the window, and lo, the minstrel stands
With a harp of silver in slender hands.

"I am come", said Cuchulain; "I hear thee sing";
He said, "Hast thou a message from Conchobar, my King?"
He said, "Hast thou a challenge of combat for me?
And, maker of sweet music, whose herald mayst thou be?"

"Son of Suailtim, 'tis thee I seek,
Whose message I must utter, His name I may not speak,
For a long way faring, the summons that I bring
It is from a greater than Uladh's King.

"I fare from farther than Emain Macha's fort;
I serve in a higher than the Red Branch court;
And thither, Cuchulain, thy journey now must be,
For the Lord of that Caiseal, He calls for thee".

This poem refers to the death of Ulster's legendary hero, Cuchulain.

"Though thy King than Conchobar be far more great,
Long for Cuchulain's coming shall He wait;
Not Rome's proud Ardrigh, the laurel-crowned,
Shall have at his feasting my Uladh's hound.

"Bard, bring homeward this answer then,
Thou hast seen me, the Hound of the Ulstermen;
Kings are my cattle, hosts my hunting-prey,
Uladh I guard until my dying day".

At that word of dying, the strange bard sighed,
And his gaze on the hero was sorrowful-eyed:
"Faithful hound of Muirtheimne's shore,
The days of thy watching are forever o'er.

"Thou must come to my King, who all kings controls,
The land of life and the place of souls,
The shield round earth and the ocean broad,
For I am the Herald of the only God:

"Death men call me; when I draw near
The lips of the mighty are blanched with fear:
So I chant no song, but with signal dumb,
To my Lord's presence I bid thee come.

"But thou, Cuchulain, has since a boy
Sought for my presence with fearless joy,
Followed my path o'er the blood-soaked ground
Where the sharp bolts of battle on shields resound.

"Therefore, O youth of the matchless steeds,
Whom bards belaud for undaunted deeds,
Thy highest praise from a chanter's breath
Is spoken now by the voice of Death".

Cuchulain answered, "I know thee now,
My comrade sworn, by my knighthood's vow;
Then say to our Lord, the whole world's King,
What gift of tribute in going shall I bring?

"There hang in my house on Dundealga's height
A hundred war-shields brazen bright,
Swords and mantles and steeds in stall
Save the Liath Macha, I would render all".

Then smiled the harper, " O son of Suailtim,
Thy great deeds for Erin were service to Him;
And in drops of thy heart's blood on Uladh's sod
Thou shalt count thy tribute to the only God".

Next day at sunset, erect, alone,
Cuchulain died by a standing stone -
Died, but fell not, with sword in hand,
And his face to the foes of the Northern land.

A Mayo Love Song

It is far and it is far
To Connemara where you are,
To where the purple glens enfold you
As glooming heavens that hold a star.

But they shall shine, they yet shall shine,
Colleen, those eyes of yours on mine,
As stars that after eve assemble
And tremble over the mountain line.

Though it be far, though it be far,
I'll travel over to where you are,
By grasslands green that lie between
And shining lakes at Mullingar.

And we shall be, yes we shall be,
Oh, colleen, lonely, beloved by me,
For evermore on a moor of Mayo,
Mid heather singing like the sea.

A WINTER SUNSET, SEEN FROM TAMNAMORE HILL OVER DERRY CITY

I - THE FOYLE VALLEY

We stand between two valleys where the high
Vault of o'erarching heaven like a rose
Flushes above yet shines not on the snows
Around us, but look westward! Look where lie
Blue peaks along a scarlet edge of sky
Whence in slow coils the blood-stained river flows,
As from some field of unimagined woes
Where heroes more than mortal fall to die;
Black shadows of a city on the red
Sea-nearing river, lie without a change
Of wind upon the water, stillness dread
Hangs brooding over it and horror strange
As if the hearts of all the world had bled
In war, behind that distant mountain range!

II - FAUGHANVALE

No single ray of sunset's reddened light
Reaches the other valley buried deep
For darkened miles between the ridges steep
Of overhanging hills, nor from the height
Comes any faintest gleam upon the white
Forsaken slopes, snow-shrouded fallen asleep
And full of dreams before the first of night;
The valley of shadows this, as that of death
And violent conflict of embattled hosts
Here is the after-world of happy ghosts
Dim Hades; lo some spirit wakeneth!
A spectral mountain peak that loometh pale
Far o'er the haunted dells of Faughanvale.

UP THE FALLS

Springtime

The spring cleanin's done,
I must pull down the blind
To keep out the sun.
Just step in and see it
From bottom to top
The place is just shinin';
Yon sofy looks fine in
The place it's been moved to;
But I'm ready to drop.

The childher, poor things,
I sent out with a warnin',
Havin' no time to dress them
For school in the mornin'.
So I bid them be off
To the waste ground to play
And with pieces all round
They're contented to stay;
If they do what they're bid
They'll get halfpence tonight,
And indeed I'm well rid
Of them out of my sight.

Such liftin' and layin'
Such scrubbin' and stitchin'.
I've whitewashed the yard,
And I've bluewashed the kitchen-
With a chair on a table
Movin' round I was able
To manage the job:
Just look at yon ceiling,
Aye, I did it myself,

But my head's fairly reelin':
Then each cupboard and shelf
I scrubbed and I papered,
And decked out wi' delf:
Them dogs and brass candlesticks
Set off the clock,
But it's not goin' now
For I gave it a knock.

Aye, them's the same curtains
Ye'd think they were new.
I starched them with yellow.
Yon one hadn't a fellow,
So I say to myself
If I cut it in two
For the head of the stair
It will just make a pair.
So ye see it looks rightly -
I thought it would do.

Just look at the room now,
Come in off the landin'.
I've turned round the bed
With the foot to the head:
And the drawers I have set
Where the wash things was standin'.
Twas a quare deal of work;
But gracious, who's yon
Come in without knockin'?
It's surely not John!
When he sees what I've done
He'll rage and he'll roar
And put the things back
Where we had them before,
And where ever he'll go,
Upstairs or below,
There'll be tracks of his boots
On my beautiful floor.

Bonnie Charlie

To the air of the Jacobite song "He will no' come back again".

Bonnie Charlie's now away,
    Past his life of toil and pain;
Other chiefs shall Ireland see,
    He will no' come back again!

CHORUS
He will no' come back again,
Never more come back again,
    Other chiefs shall Ireland see,
He will no' come back again!

Sweet the blackbird's note to me,
    Piping up the hawthorn glen;
Still one song it seems to be -
    He will no' come back again.

Chorus - He will no' come back again.

By English hate and English guile
    Many a chief of fame did fall:

Irishmen for England's smile
    Broke the truest heart of all.

'Bonnie Charlie' in this poem is Charles Stewart Parnell, leader of the Home Rule Party, who died - some say of a broken heart - after being pilloried for his affair with a married English woman, Kitty O'Shea. Alice Milligan consistently and bitterly blamed the Irish themselves, particularly the Catholic Church, for his death.

Chorus - He will no' come back again.

He trusted you as Irishmen,
      Trusted and served you rarely,
Toiled to break your slavery's chain,
      But ye were false to Charlie!

Chorus - He will no' come back again.

His dust is deep in sacred mould,
      Wept above by Ireland's skies:
His fame as deep our hearts shall hold
      Tears like rain bedim our eyes.

Chorus - He will no' come back again.

And vengeance surely shall be done,
      Ireland, by the tried and true:
These shall avenge your martyred son
      They cannot bring him back to you

Chorus - He will no' come back again.

A Winter's Night Reverie

I love the quiet of my room to gain
On some wild night of winter storms and stars
That fly as sparks from out the furnace bars;
To sit beside the rattling window pane
Besprinkled with the rolling gems of rain;
To hear the roaring of the wind that wars
With armies of the forest, whilst it mars
The blue with clouds like smoke on battle plain.
     Yet, though the very stars seem drifted by
     Before the hurricane's incessant wrath,
     They keep, I know, their old appointed path
     Above the tumult of the lower sky;
     So though dark storms of doubt from vision hide,
     Like stars above eternal truths abide.

ON THE CLIFF

The sea within the caves is roaring loud
Far, far, below the jagged ridges, where
The wind waves of the ocean of blue air
Are broken into falling foam of cloud,
That drifts and tosses on the summit proud,
And rolls o'er slopes of heath or moorland bare,
By this soft sky of summer overbowed.
The tumult of the ocean mounts not there,
  Save when the rustling fern a little space
  Is silent, comes the moaning of the sea,
  Heard faint and far from this exalted place,
  No louder than the murmur of a bee;
  But evermore, along the mountain face
  The shadows and the clouds go silently.

HEARTS DESIRE

Grania Speaks:-

    To be beautiful, to have power
    To be garmented like a flower,
    To be loved in even an hour
    By any that look upon my face;
    To make wooers of many men,
    To choose my lover but change again,
    And see him perish with longing when
    I sit proud in a queen's place

HEARTS LOVE

Beautiful Niav wonders
(Love she never knew)
If one should seek her hand at last
What she would do;
How win his choice with sweetness,
Then wound him with distain
And send him far in sorrow
But lure him back again.

. . . .

Beautiful Niav ponders
(Love she knows at last)
Watching by a window
Where one went past.
She waits to see him come again,
She thinks "I love him so -
I would be glad to die for him
Though he should never know."

THE RETURN OF LUGH
LÁMH-FHADA

Lugh Lámh-Fhada, mighty and immortal,
Lordliest of the fosterlings of Manannan mac Lir,
Far out of Erin, behind a fairy portal,
Tarried in bliss till his boyhood's ending year.
The whole world held no gladder place to dream in,
With honey of the heather fed and milk of magic cows,
Where flowers round the towers of apple-blossomed Eman
Were mingled with the burdens of heavy-fruited boughs.

And the green leaves of spring, with the gold of autumn
weather,
Were lit by the light of unending eve and morn;
For the sun and the moon stood o'er the hills together,
And looked upon the snowy vales thick-sheafed with
yellow corn.
There, in those fair, far-off, sea-sundered places,
The islands of the kingdom of the Ocean-ruler's son,
He tarried many days among the bright Dé Danaan races,
And all the wisdom of the world invisible he won.

Hosts came down from the future's misty regions,
Ghosts of buried heroes from rath and barrow flew;
And the world's long dead, with her yet unbodied legions,
Walked and talked on Aran shore with Lugh.
And they led him up to a peak upon the highland,
And bade him look unto Ocean's utmost rim
Where the faint and lovely phantom of an island,
The dwelling of his father's race, was beckoning to him.

> *Lugh Lámh-Fhada - an ancient, pre-Christian*
> *hero, half god, half human.*

And they told how of old that island had been taken,
And made the prey of plunderers - the mockery of hate,
The poor of the land by their rightful lords forsaken,
Appalled by giant tyranny, oppressed by witching fate.
And the torture of the day and the darkening of the morrow,
The woe endured in Erin's isle through all his absent years
Lugh heard of till his godlike heart was touched with
human sorrow,
And his glad immortal eyes were for the first time wet with
tears.

And the sun on high was powerless to hold him,
The moon in heaven had no might to make him stay,
So the bright Dé Danaan people flocked beach-ward to
behold him
Mount upon his magic steed and ride upon his way
O'er the high-flung, wind-swung, emerald and amber,
Over-arching, onward-marching billows of the main,
That the light, bright hoof was powerful to clamber
As swiftly as it swept the sod on Aran's smoothest plain.

And all the while in Erin's isle, the clouds of sorrow
darken;
The champion hand lets fall the brand, the lips of song are
dumb,
Or sing in wildernesses lone, since no man cares to hearken
To wonder-chimes of long-gone times, or tales of years to
come.
And the music-strings, like human things, mourn when
their masters sound them,
In lamentation wild and shrill, bewailing glories past;
And the fetters of the captives have the rust of years around
them,
And the latest-buried champion by all lips is called "the
last".

So patient necks are bowed beneath the yoke of servile
labour,
Till lo! What shining on the land? What light along the
main?

The glitter of a burnished shield, the glancing of a sabre,
And Lugh Lámh-Fhada rides in glory back again,
On the light, bright steed that was powerful to clamber,
Without breaking any bubble of the swiftly-trodden foam,
O'er the high-flung, wind-swung, emerald and amber,
Onward-sweeping, shore-ward leaping billows to his home.

And the land it lit with a strange, unearthly beauty,
And patriot strength and courage are to every heart
restored;
And boyhood leaps impatient at the trumpet-call of duty,
While maiden hands are hastening to gird him with a
sword;
For Lugh has come from the beach, where bards have
hailed him,
While cliff and rock re-echo to the sound of battle-song;
And the latest-buried warrior stands up where many wailed
him,
Arisen from the sepulchre to see them ride along.

And the world's long dead, in cairns of hill and hollow,
Have left their bones among the stones to hasten after
Lugh;
While myriads of the yet unborn the march of freedom
follow,
And the mighty lords invisible are thronging out at Brugh.
And Lugh Lámh-Fhada, the child of an immortal,
Who came with the flame of the sunburst over sea,
Leads on the host, both man and ghost, against the tyrant's
portal.
The stronghold shakes! the barrier breaks! his fatherland is
free.

AN IDYLL OF THE RED CITY

THE AWAKENING

Do you remember how, before dawn,
We were awakened by pealing notes,
By sudden outcry as of Titan voices,
Shrill, prolonged, shrieking together?

Or like chords on a vast organ
Flinging a wild chant to heaven,
Crashed in strange varying discords,
In rare, grand harmonies.

At that sounding, that summons,
Thousands in the city rose,
Groping in darkness, stumbling,
Making ready in eager haste.

We rose not for going forth,
But to watch the slowly brightening dawn
Its fading stars - and on wet pavements
The long shine of the lamps;

On every side descending
The roof-ridges of many streets,
The chimneys like battlements
Serrated everywhere around,

This poem celebrates Belfast in the 1880's, with its abundance of red brick mills and houses.

Gulfs, channels, glens of gloom,
Between cliff-like walls of buildings;
In the distance greater darkness
And confusion of shapes.

Only above the crowded town,
Roofs' lines like waves below it,
Heaving its prow among stars,
The shape of a ship.

And here and there clearly outlined,
Slender, tall, chimney towers,
No smoke from them yet,
Or freshly out-curling.

Then we watched as in every quarter
The flat-roofed mills many-windowed,
Outshining brightest constellations,
Were suddenly laced with light.

Still the notes crying, pealing
Like startled "trumpets" before battle,
Summoning in wild alarm
The help of a host.

We heard the host then coming,
The tramp, tramp of heavy feet
Of men in dingy multitudes,
Hurrying lough-ward.

Girls, women, came in groups,
In confused swift procession,
Head-shawled, gliding without talk
Towards the light of the mills.

Then the day-sun brightening,
Showed red streets in vivid glare,
Soon emptying of that crowd,
And the summoning notes ceased.

Another sounding then,
All day I overheard it,
As I strolled idly here and there,
Or read by open window.

From behind immense, trembling walls
The life-like hum where there were spinners,
And from that ship high in air
The sound of the smiting.

CUISLE MO CROIDHE

Cuisle mo croidhe, if in grief thou art,
My soul of thy grief would share a part,
Yes, I who adore thee would bear all pain for thee,
Would suffer each pang of thy aching heart
Oh love of my soul, if in grief thou art.

Cuisle mo croidhe, art thou weeping now?
Then joy shall be far from my mournful brow;
Oh! loved one and only, my days shall be lonely,
My nights shall be joyless when sad art thou,
Oh! cuisle mo croidhe, art thou weeping now?

Cuisle mo croidhe, lo! thy sorrow o'er
Then joy shall return to my life once more.
With smiles and with laughter I'll spend all hours after,
Your joy shall the light to my soul restore
Oh cuisle mo croidhe, since you weep no more.

"Cuisle mo croidhe" means "Pulse of my heart"

FADA AN LÁ

Long is the day
And lonely am I a-wishing it away;
Red morning and high noon
Fly ye quickly; but come soon
Dim twilight, for in thy light will one walk this way.

White clouds sail overhead,
But oh! I am wishing for little stars instead;
The round sun I would banish
And the green hills bid vanish
For the sake of him my delight and my dread.

"Fada an lá" means "Long is the day"

ODE FOR 6th OCTOBER

Ireland dear! through the length of my childhood lonely,
Throughout the toilsome hours of my schooling days,
No mention of thee was made unto me, save only
By speakers in heedless scorn or in harsh dispraise.
No word was told me at all of thy burdening sorrow,
No tale of thine ancient warfare yet was heard,
No whispered hope of the dawn of a brighter morrow,
Nor any news how the fight for freedom fared;
And yet in a way beyond reach of mortal knowing
To guess how ever this wonder could come to be,
As a wild flower out of a seed of God's own sowing,
Grew in my heart this flower of my love for thee.

Say did the sound of the storm-wind calling and keening,
The murmurous hush and rush in the flow of a stream,
To the ear of a listening child take a voice and a meaning?
Or was there a word that was spoken to me in a dream?
Or, hearkening unto some strain of thy music olden,
Was it my heart was enraptured and softened and stirred
By the wonder and pitiful pain of thy history, told in
The wail of a melody's notes without ever a word?
I heard thy voice like the thrill of a harp-string sighing,
Or toned like a trumpet announcing thy glory to be,
And my soul for its answer re-echoed the pledge undying,
O Ireland dear, of my whole life's love for thee!

*Charles Stewart Parnell died on the
6th October 1891*

Then since no fame of the years of thy former glory,
And never a name of one of thy kings was known,
I filled my idle hours with a fancied story
Of lords of lineage old on a shining throne.
And all thy princes were brave and thy priests were holy,
Thy queens were radiant-looked and joyous-eyed,
Thy judges, stern to the proud and just to lowly,
Brought long content to thy hills and thy plainlands wide;
And would, oh, would that now, when thou needest greatly
The hands of the brave and stalwart to set thee free,
That thou hadst the help of a host of such champions stately
As my childish fancy awakened to war for thee.

Then I was no more in those days of my happy dreaming
A helpless child, but a warrior iron-armed,
With the helmet bright on my brow, and the sharp sword beaming
Against all alien foes who thy welfare harmed.
Often o'er fields of victory, floating proudly,
I saw thy battle-flag on the breeze unfurled,
And heard the triumphant shout of an army loudly
Announce thy conquering hours to the ears of the world;
But at the end, alas! thou most sorrowful nation,
That I dared not picture a happier fate to be,
I saw thee fallen to the dust from thy lofty station,
And I was an outlaw, banned for the love of thee.

Fugitive over all hills of thine island roaming,
I faced the hail on the blast and the stinging of sleet,
I swam the turbulent waters of torrents foaming,
And waded the stones of the stream with wounded feet;
Captive brought at the last to a prison cheerless,
I drew through the lonely night, in a dungeon, breath,
And went in the chill of dawn-light, straight and fearless,
To bow on a scaffold-place my neck to death;
And, wakening out of such dreams as I loved to fashion,
I sorrowed only to know it could never be
That such a supreme last-hour should attest the passion,
O Ireland dear, and the depth of my love for thee!

Gone, and forever, the days when such dreams were;
And now, instead of the legends I fashioned alone,
The names of the patriots who in thy cause have perished,
And all thine affliction's depth, to me are known -
A burden exceeding far what my fancy framed thee,
The fettering irons weigh on thee, mother, yet,
Whilst the cowardly deed of traitor sons hath shamed thee,
And thine anguished tears are still on a gravemound wet.
Remembering why such mournful garb thou art wearing,
What wonder thy faithful sons are sad for thee,
And the hearts of the very bravest sink despairing,
O Ireland dear, of all hope to set thee free.

How, then, does hope in the depth of my heart awaken,
When time it is for the word to be uttered by none?
But even as I stood o'er the dust of the dead and forsaken,
And even when I looked on the face of thy falsest one,
Mindful of how beyond way of mortal knowing,
Undying love for thee in my child soul grew,
I hoped there would spring this flower of God's own
sowing
In the hearts of those who are strong as well as true:
And I know, though thou art fallen from thy royal station,
Ere the end of the ages come the world shall see,
In the rising dawn of thy long afflicted nation,
O Ireland dear, thy redemption come to thee!

EARTH LIGHTS

Night falling now
Here on the lonely verges of the town,
The hill lines are dark and desolate
And bird flocks cross the dreary sky.

The last shine of the sun has gone,
The world is one broad shadow,
Only in highest heaven is light,
A pallid pearly gleam.

Then stars come suddenly,
The cold, white distant stars,
Remote from even loftiest hills,
Remote from life and love.

But now more cheerful than the stars
Along the far-extending road,
The lamps fling out one by one,
Processional golden lights.

And see in many a window pane
The flash and fall of leaping fire,
Shows where in warmth of sheltered rooms
Companionship is found.

I would not be walking now
On dark slopes above the town,
Under the cold and glittering stars,
Far from the homes of men.

But I would follow the road that winds
Between the rows of cheerful lamps
Between the walls of many streets
Through the heart of the town.

And I would find among the streets
A lighted house, an opening door,
A leaping fire; and turned to me
 The face of a friend.

AT MAYNOOTH

He is a King - therefore our priests may praise him,
      Pure Nuns yield reverence, Bishops bow before,
Our Cardinal may bear to Rome his greeting
      From the Irish shore.

Homage he has from holy Patrick's Coarb,
      From him who fills the patriot Lorcan's seat,
Successors of the Saints of holy Erin,
      Who is this that you greet?

A man whose strongest claim to estimation
      Is bluff good humour, worldly commonsense
Who even to the average range of morals
      Makes no pretence.

It can be said of him "His Court is splendid,
      After the tedious length of Virtue's reign
He makes traditions of the second Charles
      Revive again".

Stern guardians of the morals of our rulers,
      Have you forgotten how in recent years
Your voices rang in wrath and commination
      In the people's ears?

This poem is a bitter attack on what Alice Milligan saw as the hypocrisy of the Roman Catholic Church. When Edward VII - no saint himself - visited Maynooth he was warmly welcomed. The same church had isolated and humiliated Parnell - ' that King uncrowned '.

Have you not thought of one who wisely led us,
     Whose sins towards Ireland were none to tell?
Yet for the sin that now you take no heed of,
     You cursed him and he fell.

You made him, while short days of life were left him,
     A man abhorred, a sinner put apart,
Till in the grave he laid the heavy burden
     Of his broken heart.

And we must wonder if this merry monarch,
     Seeing that grave episcopate around,
Smiled not in secret, thinking of their dealings
     With that King uncrowned.

THE EGOIST

"The fool hath said in his heart..."

There shall be night,
There shall be death,
There shall be nothing when I die;
There shall be silence evermore
When still am I.

There was no life,
There was no light,
There was not either night or morn;
There was no thought of anything
Till I was born.

The sun at dawn,
The moon at eve,
Rose not until I saw them rise;
Nothing has colour, nothing shape
Save in my eyes.

My death brings on the day of doom,
The earth shall fade,
The heaven shall fall;
The Universe shall pass away
 For I am all.

A Heretic

The woman speaks:
Since now you know that I love you dearly,
Tell me so that I can grasp all clearly,
The faith that you hold and the words that you say
When at noon-day bell you pause and pray.

He answered:
Listen and learn, since you love me well,
The words I speak at the noon day bell
Are spoken also at eve and morn,
The Angel's greeting ere Christ was born.

Hail unto Mary and blessed She
Above all women shall ever be;
Holy we call her and bid her pray
To God for us till our life's last day.

An Angel's words you can surely speak,
Giving praise to the Virgin meek,
And of mortals that pray for one another
Most power in prayer hath the Lord's own Mother.

No Saint moreover, no Soul in bliss,
Is banished by God, so far from this,
But they know of the strife of man with Sin
And their prayers ascend that the right may win.

I will further speak of the fast of Lent,
Of Confession due when we repent,
Of Sin absolved and of Penance needful
To make the Soul of its errors heedful.

She speaks:
These things are hard to understand,
But I look in your eyes and you hold my hand,
And love's strong bond I can keep you by,
Though Saints and Virgin I must deny.

He speaks:
Nay, then love's bond has not grace nor power
And no priest blesses the bridal hour,
Except submissive you vow to live
And your children unto the Church can give.

She answers:
Ah, then, farewell, though my heart should break,
Faith I can feign not, even for love's sake.
I plead not to Virgin nor Saint nor Martyr,
And the soul of a child I shall never barter.

Alice Milligan wrote the following six poems in memory of a very dear friend of her youth, Marjorie Arthur.

Marjorie was a fellow teacher in a ladies' school in Derry. Her mother was of the family Macdonald from the Isle of Skye.

Marjorie died very suddenly, still in her twenties, during the night of 5th February 1892.

Many years later Alice said " I spoke the name of a friend who died long, long ago, and whose memory is in all the poetry that people tell me is my best."

MARCH VIOLETS

Spring cometh up the woodland way,
  As oft of old,
When, Dear, your lips with song were gay,
  That are now so cold;
When down the greening lanes we went
  In the shine of the sun;
Or watched by banks where willows leant,
  The river run.

Blue violets you loved them best
  (Can I forget?)
Some that are dust on your dead breast
  Are treasured yet;
And these I gathered at the dawn,
  Remembering you,
Wet in the gleam of morning shone
  With tears not dew.

IF THIS COULD BE

(In memory of February 5th 1892)

If this could be
That you could come one day of life to me,
You, who are long years dead,
Where would your chosen place of meeting be,
On Scotland's shore beside a summer sea,
Or Ireland here instead?
When would you come a little time to stand
And take me by the hand?
Would you, one hour in April air your
Walk 'mid the fragrant hyacinths of Prehen,
Clouding about you in their misty blue,
Whilst greening branches threw
With fugitive alternate shadow and shine,
Or would you see Glendermot's river shore

Or strands of Fahan Mor
Bordered a league by ocean's billowy line:
Or on that hill, where long you loved to tread,
You who are long years dead;
Where harpers sang as now the heather sings
Round Aileach of the Kings,
And the wind sweeps unchallenged through the door,
Where Muircherteach of the Hostings went before,
While Cormac chanted of his travellings?
        There you would love to be
        If you could come to me.

But if the choice were mine
I would not see the billowy ocean line
Nor strands of Fahan bright
Nor Aileach wall upon the windy height.

Enough. A little room,
You swinging slowly in a rocking chair,
From firelight into gloom,
The swift gleams finding gold in your brown hair,
Your thoughtful eyes bent o'er the low-held page
Of that most honoured sage
Whose words of joyous wisdom now recall
Your accents best of all.
                This - this would be my choice,
Just to be near you - just to hear your voice,
We two together and no other near
                (Though others too are dear).
Nor would I miss the mountains and the sea
If you could come to me.

A Message

"Thou hast thought that the gift of God may be purchased with money" - St Peter to Simon the Sorcerer.

Now that I cannot have your hand to hold,
As of old,
In what way shall all I want to say
Then be told?
Are you far or are you near?
If I tell it will you hear,
Soul of my friend whose heart so long is cold?

Some there are, I know, who think when grief-distraught
That a message may be bought;
That the voice of man or woman
From beyond the veil can summon
What is sought;
While in feigned ecstatic trance
One gives cryptic utterance
To spirit thought.

But that gold should ever purchase such power to see
Cannot be.
Yet invisible and dear, if God will it you should hear
And answer me;
So if silence lasteth still
I endure, it is God's will
And I wait, tho' it be late, for the wonder that shall be.

A NOCTURNE

On a night of sorrow I cried aloud her name.
God, Who heard, said: "Hasten", and in my dream she came.
She stood; I saw her clearly by the moon's white flame;
Her eyes were sweet as ever; her voice was yet the same.

No illumining radiance lit her girlish brow -
As in life I loved her, I beheld her now;
I smiled in joy to greet her; nor did I think it strange
That death had wrought no change.

She bore with her no blossoms unknown to earthly land,
No tall white flowers of Paradise, stately and grand;
There were violets on her breast - blue violets -
And a red rose in her hand.

"How have you gathered", I asked my gentle one,
"In that unchanging region of never ceasing sun,
Where the March winds blow never, and no rain-shower ever wets
Those little violets?"

"I have had them long", she said, "I have loved them much,
They were the last flowers given my living hands to touch,
And in the fevered night of pain before my death,
Sweet was the fragrance of their breath".

"But surely you have gathered in the celestial land
That other flower which lovingly is kept in your hand?
For there is not growing here on the mountain in the snows
Any such crimson rose".

With looks of tenderest reproach my words were met.
"Dear, I have remembered! Dear, can you forget?
Seaward north of Derry, it fed on sun and dew;
It was a gift from you.

"And I shall always treasure it as priceless in worth,
God has made nothing fairer than the little flowers of earth,
As He has no more to give in His heaven above
Than your own heart's gift of never-changing love".

THE WHITE WAVE
FOLLOWING

(Written on a voyage through the Hebrides. In Memory of Marjorie Arthur)

Like the white wave following
Our ship through changing waters,
The memory of your love is
In life that alters.
The clouds pass over head,
And like clouds the islands
Flock up - and hurrying on
Float by on the blue of ocean:
The sun goes, and the moon,
Along many mountains
Amid changing stars,
Into heaven uprolling,
New lochs and lands
In each hour illumines:
And all waves of the sea,
Tide-swept and wind-swayed
From morning unto night,
Move ceaselessly by us.

But against all winds
And all swift tide-races,
To all lochs and lands
And sea-girt lonely places,
Sunlit and moonlit,
Heaving and hollowing
Through wind-gleam, and glass-calm,
Comes one white wave following.

And like that white wave
In the sun-lit sound of Jura,
Like that wave, bright-crested
Amid grey seas by Sanda,
On black rocks breaking
Around distant Rona,
Or in foam-track fading
O'er a sea of slumber
As we came from Canna
To Skye of your kindred:
> Like that white wave, following
> The ship through changing waters,
> The memory of your love is
> In life that alters.

LYRICS IN MEMORY OF A SEA LOVER

A WINTER WALK

Dear! though in the House of God your dwelling now
must be;
Yet, if memory endures with immortality,
You must still remember the day you walked with me,
'Neath the cold sky of winter, to find the Northern Sea.

Clear rang our footsteps out, iron hard the road,
The chill of snow was in the air, and yet it had not snowed.
And the red sky of sunset, through branches bare,
Shed a frosty radiance on your nut-brown hair.

But ere ever to the river mouth at Culmore we came.
Faded out of heaven quite was the sunset flame.
And the first stars of twilight shone o'er the hill tops high.
So back again towards Derry we turned with a sigh.

And as with hurrying steps we walked beneath darkening
skies,
The lights of the city burst upon our eyes:
Rank on shining rank of flame, a pyramid of light,
From the brink of Foyle River to the crest of Derry's
height.

But amid those galaxies of lustrous heaven and hill
One light in thoughtful silence kept you watching still -
A ship-light moving slowly to the river bar.
That to your homeward yearning heart was fairer than a
star.

Pointing to the gliding hull, the seething foam,
"There goes the ship", you said, "that bears me home".
Your voice thrilled sweetly tender, your eyes grew tearful
bright,
"And would", you said, "that I might sail to Scotland's
shore to-night".

Ah, it was not numbered then among the future's fears
That, ere the ending of two swift-passing years,
The vessel that you looked on then - while the smile came
to your lips -
Would bear you seaward to your grave from Derry of the
ships.

WHY DERMOT CAME ASHORE

"Dermot! Dermot MacNamara,
    Will you launch your boat from shore?
See how fast the clouds are flying,
    Hear the wind and waters roar!
All the boats within the harbour
    Dance at anchor on the tide;
If it's rough within, oh, Dermot!
    It is rougher far outside".

Dermot looked across the water,
    Jumped into the fishing craft,
Looked to where the storm was raging,
    Wildly raging, looked and laughed.
Now his boat is lightly lifted
    On a green wave's smoking crest;
Now 'tis hidden in the hollow,
    Rocked about on ocean's breast.

Mary, with a shawl about her,
    Stood upon the fishing pier;
All her dark hair hung disordered,

    In her eye there shone a tear.
"Dermot! Dermot MacNamara!
    Do not loose your boat from shore;
If you sail beyond the harbour
    We shall never meet you more.

"Leave alone the nets and salmon,
    Leave alone the lobster creels;
Father's coat is off and drying,
    By the hearth he warms his heels.
Tim and Con are gone a courtin',

Not a man of all the crew
Takes a thought about the fishin',
        Dermot! Dermot, why should you?"

Dermot looked at her a moment
        With a kind of dawning hope,
Then from out the ring of iron
        Quickly drew the fastening rope.
"Tim and Con are happy, chattin'
        With their sweethearts fair and kind;
I have not a girl to love me,
        Best for the nets to mind.

"Since you say you will not wed me,
        It's no matter if I'm drowned;
Troth, there won't be many weepin'
        When on shore my corpse is found".
"Dermot", answered Mary, softly,
        "Do not loose the boat from shore;
Every child about would miss you,
        For your jokes they'd miss you sore.

"Not a man in all the village
        Has as strong an arm to row;
Father couldn't do without you
        Dermot! Dermot, do not go!"
Mary's eyes are wet with weeping,
        So she looks the other way;
And the billows break about her,
        Drenching her with drifted spray.

Dermot's out upon the water,
        Loud above the waves he spoke:
"Shall I stay to please the childer,
        Dance the jig or make the joke?
Though my arm is strong, your brother
        Soon will learn as well to row;
If there's nothing else to keep me,
        Fare you well, for I must go".

"Dermot", Mary answered, "Dermot,
    Come back, darlin' to the shore;
Sure, if you were dead and drowneded,
    I would never smile no more.
Loud I'd weep as any widow,
    Weep until my heart would break;
Come back, Dermot MacNamara,
    For your lovin' Mary's sake".

Quickly Dermot MacNamara
    With the back stroke plies the oar,
Comes across the raging water,
    Stands upon the rocky shore:
To the rusty ring of iron
    Ties the rope with hasty hands;
Hurries up the slippery pier steps,
    Gains the place where Mary stands.

Mary pulls her shawl around her,
    Shyly tries her tears to hide;
Dermot takes her hand and gently
    Puts the sheltering shawl aside.
At their feet the waves are splashing,
    Mary doesn't heed them more -
Nothing heeds but Dermot's whisper,
    "For a kiss I came ashore!"

WHEN I WAS A LITTLE GIRL

When I was a little girl,
In a garden playing,
A thing was often said
To chide us, delaying:

When after sunny hours,
At twilight's falling,
Down through the garden walks
Came our old nurse calling -

"Come in ! for it's growing late,
And the grass will wet ye!
Come in! or when it's dark
The Fenians will get ye".

Then, at this dreadful news,
All helter-skelter,
The panic struck little flock
Ran home for shelter.

And round the nursery fire
Sat still to listen,
Fifty bare toes on the hearth,
Ten eyes a-glisten -

To hear of a night in March,
And loyal folk waiting
To see a great army of men
Come devasting -

An army of Papists grim,
With a green flag o'er them,
Red-coats and black police
Flying before them.

But God (Who our nurse declared
Guards British dominions)
Sent down a deep fall of snow
And scattered the Fenians.

"But somewhere they're lurking yet,
Maybe they're near us",
Four little hearts pit-a-pat
Thought "Can they hear us?"

Then the wind-shaken pane
Sounded like drumming;
"Oh!" they cried, "tuck us in,
The Fenians are coming!"

Four little pairs of hands,
In the cots where she led those,
Over their frightened heads
Pulled up the bedclothes.

But one little rebel there,
Watching all with laughter,
Thought "When the Fenians come
I'll rise and go after".

Wished she had been a boy
And a good deal older -
Able to walk for miles
With a gun on her shoulder;

Able to lift aloft
That Green Flag o'er them
(Red coats and black police
Flying before them);

And, as she dropped asleep,
Was wondering whether
God, if they prayed to Him
Would give fine weather.

A WHITE FLOWER

No lilies of the valley are pure enough to place
Within my true love's fingers or near her tranquil face,
For she who in the summer, when garden plots were gay,
Walked down among the lilies, lies paler now than they.

No white dove in its wheeling, where skies are blue above,
No song-bird in its soaring, ah! swift soul of my love;
No swallow in its sweeping to summer over sea,
Hath yet out-dared in distance this heavenward flight of
thee!

To-morrow when they leave thee deep laid beneath the
mould,
And come to pace in sorrow, when twilight skies are cold,
The lonely garden alleys, oh! loved one of my heart,
I'll think the faintest star of heaven is nearer than thou art.

And yet no fair bird folding its wings upon my breast,
No lily laid to wither where once thou were caressed,
No star-beam bearing purely from heaven to earth its light,
May come as near me as thou art, soul of my soul to-night!

White flower from God's own garden, white dove from
heavenly nest!
A thought of thee shall keep the heart, where once was
made thy rest.
White as the graveyard mound shall be that thou art laid
below
In summer time with lilies, in winter with the snow.

A BENEDICTION

Dear little boy,
Soft-handed, playing with white daisies now,
Playing above tree shadows on the grass
Where sorrowful I pass,
A gloom upon the sunlight of your joy
Seems to fall down whilst I am laying now
A kiss upon the brightness of your brow,
For with that kiss I did not wish you joy,
Dear little boy.

But this I wish for you,
Not fortune, not much ease, not blissful days,
Not overmuch of even well-won praise.
Not even at end of life your labours' due -
But that beneath those little faltering feet,
In sacrifice complete,
A hard path may be chosen, the upward way,

On which I pause to-day -
Pause, helpless, weary, and can walk no more,
Whose work in life is o'er.

And I bequeath,
When I must rest my share of earth beneath,
My days of toil being done,
The hope of this so nearly hopeless heart
To you, weak little one,
To be cherished and held apart,
Perhaps by failure to be tried and shaken,

*Addressed to her youngest brother, Charles,
twenty-two years her junior.*

53

Yet not by you forsaken,
But kept, as I have kept it, handed on
Till, when you too are dust beneath the flowers
Triumph at last is ours,
When darkness yields to the dawn;
And may it be our best of heaven to know
That God has made it so.

Now you may run,
White-pinafored, into the spreading sun;
'Mid shadows racing as the clouds pass by,
Go, play; as thoughtless as the butterfly,
The white, gay thing that you are chasing after,
With ringing childish laughter;
And I, whose innocent days of mirth are o'er,
Seeing you look to me and laugh again,
Feel hope steal back into my heart once more -
Hope, with this thought of pain,
That, oh! you would be frightened if you knew
All I have wished for you.

IN THE WIRRAL

(To Ita, who returned to Ireland, August 4th, 1916)

From gay, blood-guilty London
You've travelled fast and far,
And well can I picture
The place where now you are;
And gladly would I follow
On the way that you went,
But old friendship holds me here -
Not ill content.

Why should I hasten,
With harebells still here;
I missed their frail beauty
In the earlier year:
You missed your garden's glory
When summer blooms were gay,
Because of one death-fated
Who all the summer waited
His death's sure day.

> *This poem was written just after the execution of Sir Roger Casement in London, for his part in the Easter Rising of 1916. He and Alice were good friends. The execution is referred to in the second last verse. Many Irish prisoners of the Easter Rising were held in Wales. 'Ita' was Ita McNeill of Cushendun, the Nationalist sister of Ronald McNeill, a prominent Unionist.*

Now we tread the heather
On paths far apart,
Here the sturdy bracken grows
Higher than my heart,
And the scarlet berries cluster
On the slender rowan tree;
You walk beside Dunlewy lake
And I by sands of Dee.

Through the sea silver
I watch the shoals emerge,
Laying their golden steps
Across the ebbing surge,
Where o'er smoke drift and furnace flare
The sunset glows and pales,
Above the high hills that guard
The holiest well in Wales.

Many a grey castle
Stands there grim and proud,
And soaring Moel-famman
Looks fair beneath a cloud,
Whilst ghost-like in grandeur
When heaven shineth clear,
'Mid the marvels of morning
Shall Snowdon appear.

You see scattered cabins
Amid the granite rocks,
Barefooted children
Herding woolly flocks:
Here are stately mansions
Whose gardens beneath
Throw their rosy garlands
Around the purpling heath.

How from England's beauty
Can I my heart withhold?
By thinking of her crowds that cheered
When a death bell tolled;
And the mountains of Wales there,
For all they look so kind,
Guard many an Irish mother's son
Whom I have much in mind.

So though old friendship holds me
With a claim I can't forget,
Ere they reap the oats in Ulster
I'll cross to Ireland yet,
And bide a while in Donegal
Where the priests are kind as wise,
And for your cause of sorrow
There are tears in manhood's eyes.

TO THE MOST BEAUTIFUL

(The tribute of an aspiring poet with a limited income)

"Helen in a sailor hat
Is a sight to wonder at,
A matchless beauty to adore,
A picture I could kneel before!
That simple head-dress she can please in
Beyond all belles at London's season,
Decked in the plumes and lappets gay.
Chiffons, feathers, flowers and laces
Go with other sorts of faces,
Toning down the features faulty
Like taking rhymes in poems halty.
Helen, needing none of that,
Queens it in her sailor hat.

Helen in her holland gown
Is the talk of all the town,
Envied of less lovely others,
Cause of rage to aunts and mothers.
And though I've heard at race and ball
Her dainty gowns outrival all,
Methinks that thus when plainly dressed
She triumphs more than all the rest.
Frills and flounces are *de rigeur*
With less perfection of a figure,
Often hiding obvious angles

With well placed folds and cloth in tangles
Veiling that with skilled illusion.
But Helen's form is so complete

From stately head to pretty feet
She wins the praise of all the town
Decked in her simple morning gown
As forth she walks with step sedate
Under the trees from Albert Gate."

So sings our artful friend the poet,
His moral, could fair Helen know it,
Is simply this: through all pretence
Be beautiful at small expense.

THE VALIANT-HEARTED GIRL

"When the hours of daylight dwindle in the autumn of the
year,
They would have me take the spindle, who am longing for a
spear,
And they call me from my comrades' game of battle in the
fern
To tarry where the maidens of my mother turn a quern.
Now must the needle-scorner be a broiderer of smocks,
A bridal robe adorner, and a wreather of my locks,
A longer for a lover and a smiler at a glass,
Who had rather gaze o'er ocean-ways where gusty shadows
pass?
Must I shoot no more my curragh in a furrow of the deep,
But sit to rock the cradle for my baby brother's sleep,
And sigh to know that he may grow to tower in battle's van,
Whilst I shall bide at home to weep because I'm not a man?

Now, Donal, quit thy laughter! Look me straight and
answer true,
When the deer was hastened after, when the wood we
hurried through,
Who was it went most boldly past the grey wolf's lurking
place
At the thicket in the hollow? Who to follow in the chase
Was still the fleetest footed? Who stood ready with the dart
When the moment came to shoot it to the panting creature's
heart
As she turned on her pursuer at the crag above the glen?
It was I alone who slew her, who will slay no deer again;
For I wept to see her wounded and I sobbed to watch her
die,
And I'd never make a soldier, you declared with mocking
eye;

But I'd kill my country's foeman, though I wept above a deer,
For this heart that melts with pity, boy, shall never melt with fear.

Oh, weary lot of womankind! Thrice wearier to me,
Knowing I have the strength of mind a warrior to be!
Knowing that battlefields are lost where cowards turn to fly
For lack of some loud rallying call, such as these lips could cry!
Knowing that Conal's clan may pine in want of such a chief
As I would make, if I were not a woman, to my grief!
Oh, tell me, white-haired poet, for thou'rt wiser than the priest,
And well I love to listen to thy chanting at the feast;
Thou art rich in wisdom of the world and learned in lore divine,
And hardest riddles thou canst read, then prithee answer mine;
If I may not swing a battle-axe and must not march to war,
What has God in heaven, who made me, made me valiant-hearted for?"

Tumbling all the nut-brown tresses on the forehead of the child
With his heavy hands caresses, slow the poet spake and smiled -
Smiled to see that face uplifted and the reverent, hopeful eyes,
For she deemed him heavenly gifted, and she dreamed him more than wise,
"Thou must take", he said, "the spindle, thou must put away the spear,
And as hours of daylight dwindle, to thy mother giving ear,
Must forsake thy boy-companions at their battles in the fern,
For thy playing time is over now, and time has come to learn
All such duties as with beauty's dower when known shall make thee famed

At council board where fittling brides for kingly youths are named.
Now never toss that dimpled chin, nor shake denying hair,
For the Lord who make thee valiant, child, hath made thee also fair!

So fair thou art, that where thou art, in wondering throngs shall be
The noblest wooers in the land to tender court to thee:
But all their sighs those laughing eyes shall make a mockery of,
Until that young unconquered heart yields to the conqueror Love.
Then thou shalt wed, methinks, some prince of earth's most royal line,
None but a kingly warrior's soul could dare to mate with thine.
And, oh, be sure thy strength at length shall stand thee well in need
When comes a day for him to mount his prancing battle steed:
For men must go at duty's call, whilst women bide to wait
Through length of agonising hours, the uncertain stroke of fate.
And thou shalt learn, if cold and dead they carry him from war,
What God, who frameth women's hearts, hath given them courage for!"

Oh, the scornful look she gave him! Oh, the pride of her reply!
"Has God given us courage only to behold our dearest die?
Has he granted strength and patience that we calmly may endure
Those oppressions of this Nation's that our praying cannot cure?
Methinks, oh, white-haired poet, thou art foolish as the priest,
Who knoweth nothing of the heart - of woman's heart at least!

What comfort is in strength allowed to only shed the tear?
What help in courage merely called to bow above the bier?
If comes a day when, as you say, I'll mourn a warrior low,
One pain beyond all pain, one thought above all thoughts of
woe
Shall torture me with wild regret; to think! to think!" she
said,
"That I went not by my true love's side and died not in his
stead!"

MERELY PLAYERS

(To S ..... A Memory of Tableaux and a Play).

Memory holds a girlish picture of you,
Kneeling, with a Celtic cross above you,
Under the saintly Brigid's cloak of blue;
Innocent and fair to all beholders,
With your rippling hair about your shoulders,
When we staged the drama of Red Hugh.

So when came your hour of heaviest sorrow,
Words of mine your prayerful lips could borrow;
Prayer for such deliverance as he knew,
Who from Dublin on a night of snowing
Fled with his companions, onward going
Over hills and vales of Wicklow through.

And of late Saint Brigid's feast-day found you,
With your little children clustering round you,
Nigh those hills that sheltered our Red Hugh;
Did you dream then, ere a day departed,
You would smile exultant, happy-hearted,
And the whole sad land rejoice with you?

*This poem is dedicated to Sinéad, wife of
Eamonn de Valéra. Her husband was
imprisoned in Lincoln Prison after the Easter
Rising, but escaped on 3rd February, 1919.
Alice is recalling her own play,* The Escape of
Red Hugh, *in which Sinéad was an actress.*

THE LONELY ROAD

Now we have said "Farewell" my friend,
After the parting pain,
Turn your face to the lonely road,
And look not back again.

> Set your feet on the narrow track
> That runneth to the sea,
> And bow your head to the will of God,
> And think no more of me.

For oh! my friend, if you looked back
But only once again,
I would stretch out my arms to you,
And you would know my pain.

> And you would come to me, my love,
> And hold me to your heart;
> And if but once your lips touched mine,
> Oh! we could never part.

Then, since it is the will of God
That this is best to be,
Turn your face to the lonely road,
And think no more of me.

TO SEUMAS IN MONTANA

(On receiving a card from him at Butte, Montana, "A Mile in Air", signed with his name, and that of the brother of a dead friend, of whom I have written in my poems "A Nocturne", "A White Wave Following" and "A Winter Walk".)

Oh! friend far away,
Welcome was the word that came from you to-day,
Wonderful the news of that "Mile in Air" meeting,
And the name that came after the Gaelic of your greeting.
To think you've met with Donald of the brown hair curled
On the ridge of the world.

How came you two, Brother and lover of the dearest ones I knew
(Marjorie of the White Wave and Ethna of the Songs),
How came you together 'mid the world's jostling throngs?
Oh! surely to this meeting, oh! surely ye were led.
By soft voices of the dead.

For 'tis many a lonely year
Since from Marjorie's folk came any news or cheer,
And often I was longing for the silence to break,
For the dear ones of my dead have been dear for her sake.
And often I was thinking, when I looked across the sea,
In Scotland of the Lough lands have they forgotten me?

So, far-away friend,
Welcome, thrice welcome, the word that you send,
And 'tis many a time since my life-work did begin,
That help came from you and from one of your kin,
So take thanks for the news you sent, the half-world round,
From the marvellous mountains where Donald you found.

IN THE ZOO

(To Donal and Dermot, sons of Jack Morrow, November, 1918)

Oh children, little children laughing gaily
At the great wild creatures in the Zoo:
At the bears in pits and cages,
Lions, tigers in their rages,
You must wonder that I cannot laugh with you.

But the white wolf, he whimpers for the forest,
For the ice-floe moans the polar bear,
And the eagle, the angry golden eagle,
Has wings meant to spread in azure air.

So looking through the bars that here confine them,
Dear children, I cannot laugh with you;
For I'm thinking of another place in Dublin
Where men are in cages too.

TILL FERDIA CAME

(Written during a time of civil strife in Ireland 1922-23).

We read it in that ancient tale,
The glory of the Northern Gael;
How young Cuchulain's single sword
Stemmed the advance of Connacht's horde,
And one by one the champions fell
On Ulla's border guarded well;
Battle he deemed a joyous game
Till to the ford Ferdia came.

For as he rested on his blade,
Waiting new contest, undismayed,
Counting the roll of vanquished proudly,
He heard a trumpet challenge loudly,
And from the invading army's rank
A chief strode towards the river bank;
Cuchulain's hand shook on his sword
As Ferdia faced him at the ford.

Swift on his proud lips died the smile;
('Twas Maeve had planned this deed of guile)
The battle joy that fired his glance
Faded before the uplifted lance
Of Ferdia, his more than brother,
His comrade chosen before all other,
In many a feat of danger tried
And trusted, at Cuchulain's side
Since boyhood, when each martial sport
They learned at Scathach's island fort
Now to a strife, that was no game,
Against his friend Ferdia came.

Cuchulain's trust was not betrayed
Spite of the trap Queen Maeve had laid;
To recreant friendship all untender
He steeled his heart - our land's defender
And, after contest long had sped,
He launched at last the gae-bolg dread,
And stricken sore, Ferdia dying,
Clasped in the arms that slew was lying,
Whilst Ulster's champion, bending low,
Uttered his grief in chant of woe,
"Oh, battle was a gladsome thing
Till to the ford Ferdia came!"

And in these days of blood and tears
The words re-echo in my ears,
As many a comrade yields his life
To former friend in desperate strife;
I think of Collins in the West,
The life blood clotted on his breast:
And like enough the hand that slew him
Not long before pledged fealty to him,
With many another fighting man
Linked to the cause Republican;
And when through Dublin's street they bore him,
Draping the flag in honour o'er him,
We mourned to think of other days:
His fearless feats, his merry ways.
"Death was a jest, the fight a game
Till to the ford Ferdia came".

My grief for Childers, Boland too,
And, oh, unconquered Cahal Brugha,
When reeling through the lurid flame
Still armed, defiant still you came
To fall where oft your speech had rung
In accents of our native tongue;
You shed your blood on Dublin street
Where oft, towards festive hall your feet

Had walked in happy company
With lads, who lived this sight to see.
A foreign mandate forced the game
Against Cuchulain, Ferdia came.

Oh grief! of griefs beyond all other,
Two valiant sons of one fond mother;
Two brothers, pledged in Ireland's righting,
In severed ranks were sternly fighting
In cause opposed: and yet - oh yet
Thank God for this - they had not met.
The deepest, darkest deed of all
Might have befallen - did not befall
Yet - Brian fell by hand of brother

(Some hapless son of Ireland - Mother)

Where battlemented mountains sweep
To end in famed Ben Bulben's steep,
Where Angus raised his cries of woe
O'er the Fianna long ago!
Like Diarmuid wounded by the boar,
When Druid skill could not restore.
His mangled form they brought away
To lay it in Kilbarrack's clay,
And sundered kindred meet to kneel
Above the grave of Brian MacNeill.
As martyr some are praying o'er him,
As erring rebel some deplore him;
No bitterer tears I deem were poured
O'er Ferdia at the Slaughter ford.

Oh brothers! Sons of one loved land,
Who to such combat armed each hand,
What cause of fury and of hate
Had either? By what mocking fate
Are ye, begirt with scornful foes,
Now locked in self-destructive throes,
Whilst they, in calm complacence jeering,
Wait our annihilation nearing;
Wishful that after all your toils,
Of Victory they will reap the spoils.

They tell us in that noble tale,
The glory of the Northern Gael,
When weary of the watch he'd kept
And wounded sore, Cuchulain slept;
The youth of Erin glad, untired,
With hearts untamed, with hopes inspired,
Rose up aginst the invading foe.
As it was then it may be so
In these sad days of blood and tears.
Have faith - trust God for happier years,
For strength upheld, for peace restored
'Twixt those who battle at the ford.

IN THE LAKELANDS

(Rosses, Co Donegal)

My love dwells by Gweebarra of the surges,
But here among the lakes my home must be,
Here where at dawn for daylight's earliest showing,
My eyes look forth - for shine upon the sea -
Here where I sit to watch the water flowing,
And with its going long to rise and flee.

Great is the hurry on you rushing water -
There is no need for such a race to be -
The hills are happy with your tinkling laughter,
The hills that never hear the laugh o' me.
Oh, running brooks, 'tis you I'd follow after,
Down to the barren shore and bitter sea.

But like a lake enlocked among the mountains,
With no brook course to let its waters free,
The rocks that wall the lakes among the mountains
Here in the strong Rosses prison me.
O, to be fleeing like the flowing water
Down to Gweebarra and my love with me.

A Song of Freedom

In Cavan of the little lakes,
As I was walking with the wind,
And no one seen beside me there,
There came a song into my mind:
It came as if the whispered voice
Of one, but none of human kind,
Who walked with me in Cavan then,
And he invisible as wind.

On Urris of Inish-Owen,
As I went up the mountain side
The brook that came leaping down
Cried to me - for joy it cried;
And when from off the summit far
I looked o'er land and water wide,
I was more joyous than the brook
That met me on the mountain side.

To Ara of Connacht's isles,
As I went sailing o'er the sea,
The wind's word, the brook's word
The wave's word, was plain to me -
"As we are, though she is not,
As we are, shall Ireland be -
There is no King can rule the wind,
There is no fetter for the sea".

QUESTIONS

A Child speaks:
      Was all the same
      Before I came,
      Before I saw,
      Before I knew?
      Before I answered to my name
      Was the grass green
      Or the sky blue?
      I can't think how they were;
      Can you?

A Man thinks:
      Will it be so
      After I go?
      Blue heaven above
      Wide earth below
      One that I love
      Long years may be
      Mourning for me,
      But will I know?

Index